David's Tree

Barbara Niffenegger

Balboa Press books may be ordered through booksellers or by contacting:

Balboa Press
A Division of Hay House
1663 Liberty Drive
Bloomington, IN 47403
www.balboapress.com
1 (877) 407-4847

ISBN: 978-1-9822-3668-7 (sc)
ISBN: 978-1-9822-3669-4 (e)

Print information available on the last page.

Balboa Press rev. date: 10/30/2019

BALBOA.PRESS

Barbara Niffenegger

DAVID'S TREE

Summer tree Backyard

DEDICATED TO DAVID AND GARY

My twin inspirations who love trees and what
they do for us "two-legged" people.

David and Gary in front of lake 1994

Gary and David Running in back yard 1993

Also dedicated to all those who love nature, forests
and our natural beauty around us!

THIS IS A STORY OF RESILIENCE. THE MESSAGE
FORM THE LITTLE TREE IS NEVER GIVE UP, BE
PRESISTENT AND BE A FRIEND TO ALL!

It was Arbor Day and David had a gift for his mother. David and Gary knew their mother would like the gift. The gift was alive. He carried his gift home carefully wrapped in a damp paper towel, newspapers and a loving hand that held it securely.

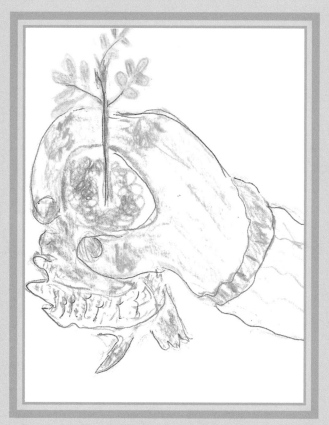

Hand Holding a sapling tree.

The wind was blowing and it had turned cool. It was a day of billowing gray clouds that looked like winter had returned. David protected his gift by holding it close to his body. He and his twin brother, Gary, hurried home because it was getting cold.

School to home with trees and wind.

When David and Gary got home, David held the gift behind his back. He and Gary walked up behind their Mother and said in unison, "We have a gift for you!!" Their Mother clapped her hands in excitement. "Let me see!"

David with tree behind his back and his Mom.

David took the gift carefully from behind his back. It was a little tree. A little ash tree. David's Mother said, "I have the perfect place to plant the tree."

David giving tree to his Mom.

David, Gary and their Mother went to get a shovel. Then they went to the backyard. There they dug a hole for the tree by the back fence. They put small rocks around the tree to mark it's place. Then they watered the tree.

David, Gary and their Mom planting the tree in the back yard.

David and Gary's Mother said that the tree will grow taller than them!
Next week, David and Gary went to check on the tree. It was
nowhere to be found! Even the little rocks were gone!
David and Gary ran inside to get their Mother. Their Mother said, "I'm
SURE the tree is there. Let's go look closely!

David and Gary's Older Brother Mowing

Outside they all went and looked really closely. The tree WAS there but it was only two inches high! It had no leaves. David and Gary's older brother had mowed the tree down when he cut the grass!

Photo: Back yard picture with David, Gary and their older brother.

David, Gary and older brother making fence around the tree.

David and Gary's mother said that the tree would be
ok. It would still be taller than them someday!
The little tree was mowed down 2 more times!! Then their older
brother helped them build a little fence around the tree!

A year past. The tree did grow six inches and it grew nine leaves which turned yellow in the fall. They dug up the three and put it in a small pot. They were moving to a different house.

Little Tree with fence

Porch with plants

They took the tree to their new house and put it on the front porch with a lot of other plants. One day a strong wind blew the little tree and it's pot into a neighbor's shrubs against their house. When David and Gary were going to plant the tree, they couldn't find it!!!

Two months later, the neighbor found it in the shrubs by his house. It was ok!

Deer eating tree and tree with birds

David and Gary planted the tree in the back yard where it could be seen from the kitchen window and their bedroom window. The tree like the spot. Deer, birds and other animals visited it. A deer took a bite out of the top of the tree. But the tree liked the spot so well it grew 10 inches that year!

David, Gary and older brother on front steps with Little Tree in pot on porch.

The next year, David and Gary moved into another house. Their older brother was going to Virginia Tech. Again, they took the tree. This time it had to go in a large pot. When they got to their new house, the tree was left in the pot and was on the front porch.

Cindy the Cat by pot with tree.

A neighbor's cat, named Cindy, would come and lay by the tree to nap and watch birds. The tree liked Cindy. It grew five inches this year!

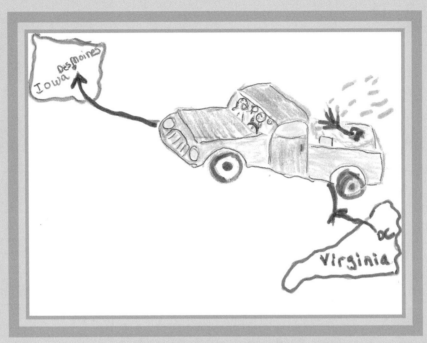

Virginia to Iowa and Truck

The next year, David, Gary and their parents would move from Virginia to Iowa. They would take David's tree along. Again, the tree was moved in its big pot. It traveled in the back of their Dad's pick-up truck. The wind blew all the leaves from the limbs of the tree as it travelled half way across the United States.

In Iowa, at Grandma's, the tree was planted in the back
yard where it can be seen from the kitchen window.

Animals and ball player in the backyard.

Birds, rabbits, squirrels, raccoons, a fox and a Bald Eagle visited the tree. David, Gary and their friends played baseball by the tree.

The tree grew as tall as David and Gary as their mother told them it would.
Someday it will be taller than David and Gary and will give a lot of shade.
It is a special gift!

Little tree in back yard after grown to 8- foot tree.

SEASONS WITH THE TREE!

SPRING 2012

Tree in SPRING

SUMMER 2012

Tree in SUMMER

FALL 2002

Tree in FALL

WINTER 2019

Tree in Winter

Help save our Green Ash Trees.

This story takes place from Virginia to the Iowa. Iowa lost most of the Green Ash trees in the late 1969-2000. Moving firewood from one location to the other was a major point of what NOT to do. This is still a NOT TO DO! Get your firewood if you are a camper from the location you are going to. DO NOT HAUL FIRE WOOD FROM ONE LOCATION TO THE OTHER. PLEASE!!!!!

Go on line to the Department of Natural Resources (in the West and Mid-West) and Forestry Service in the East and Southern States. As recently as September 2019, information has been shared television in Virginia about the Emerald Ash Borer. Little Tree has escaped (so far) the Emerald Ash Borer! It is up to YOU to help. Learn what a Green Ash looks like. Identify if you have one. Go on line and see what you can do to save the trees. Talk to your city planners. Seek information from the Extension Services in your state. Google emerald ash borer for more information. Learn about what you should do to help any of your trees to keep them healthy. We take for granted our trees when we should not. They hold our soil. Give us shade and protection. They provide food for us and for the animals who count on them for survival. Being in Virginia, the forests are one of our best natural resources. Thank you!!!!

OLEACEAE

Green Ash
Fraxinus pennsylvanica lanceolata
Leaf form: pinately compound
          opposite
Fruit type: winged (1-seeded
          samaras in open paniculate
          clusters)

Green Ash Leaves and Seeds from my personal leaf collection from the 1970's (I am an Earth Science Major from Drake University, Des Moines, Iowa. BSED in 1966. Was a Science Consultant, Teacher, and Trainer in Fairfax County, VA for several years. Graduated from the Virginia Tech Danforth Foundation, Leadership and Administration in 1996.

Several things you can do for you, your children and your environment and others!

1. Volunteer
2. Help clean up a park, a city block, a school grounds, etc.
3. Learn about your environment—go on line and learn about the environment from many sources.
4. Visit and work with your National Parks, State Parks, Local Parks and how you can help.
5. Work with 4-H, Boy Scouts, Girl Scouts
6. Go to a "Pick your own" –berries, apples, pumpkins, etc.
7. Frequent your local farmer's market
8. Get to know and purchase items from your local farmers, ranchers
9. Visit local farms when the opportunity present themselves
10. Create an environment for bees, butterflies, and other wildlife. (Criteria is on National Wildlife Federation's Website.)
11. Go to your Extension Bureau at you State University. Find out what they can offer you.
12. Sit outside in silence for 10-15 minutes daily –JUST BE!!!
13. Enjoy crickets, tree frogs, and other natural sounds.
14. If an animal crosses the road in front of you, <u>slow down—save a life!!</u>
15. Turn off your electronics for a minimum of 1 hour a day—use your time to relax!
16. BE KIND NOT ONLY DAILY BUT MAKE IT YOUR MISSION!
17. SAY THANK YOU TO OTHERS WHEN EVER THE OPPORTUNITY ARISES!
18. MAKE IT YOUR MISSION TO SAY THANK YOU TO THOSE WHO PROTECT US—OUR POLICE, FIRE AND ALL OF OUR FIRST RESPONDERS.
19. Only 1% of our population SERVE, HONOR and PROTECT in the Military. Do not only THANK THEM FOR THEIR SERVICE, also thank them for THEIR FAMILIES' sacrifice.
20. MEDITATE. Be in the NOW. Relax.
21. Turn off your cell as you travel—Move Over when you see people, First Responders, animals on the margin of the road—SLOW DOWN and relax and be aware of your surroundings.
22. Say THANK YOU!

Printed in the United States
By Bookmasters